The House of Straw

Also by Carmen Bugan

Poetry

Crossing the Carpathians (Carcanet/Oxford*Poets*, 2004)

Prose

Burying the Typewriter (Picador, 2012)
Seamus Heaney and East European Poetry in Translation:
        Poetics of Exile (Legenda/Maney Publishing, 2013)

Carmen Bugan

The House of Straw

Shearsman Books

First published in the United Kingdom in 2014 by
Shearsman Books
50 Westons Hill Drive
Emersons Green
BRISTOL
BS16 7DF

Shearsman Books Ltd Registered Office
30–31 St. James Place, Mangotsfield, Bristol BS16 9JB
(this address not for correspondence)

www.shearsman.com

ISBN 978-1-84861-324-9

Acknowledgements
Versions of most poems in this collection have appeared in *Harvard Review, PN Review, Modern Poetry in Translation, The Balliol College Record, Wolfson College Record, Branch-Lines: Edward Thomas and Contemporary Poetry, See How I Land: Oxford Poets and Exiled Writers: an Anthology, Seam, Oxford Magazine, Oxford Poetry, Romulus, Big Scream, International Literary Quarterly, Joining Music with Reason: 34 Poets, British and American, Oxford 2004-2009 chosen by Christopher Ricks,* and *HazMat Review.* 'Visiting the country of my Birth' has won a commendation in the 2011 National Poetry Competition (UK) and appears on the Poetry Society's webpage as well as in my memoir *Burying the Typewriter.* Thanks are due to the Hawthornden International Retreat for Writers where, as a Fellow, I spent a month working on parts of this manuscript. Most of this collection owes its existence to a generous grant from the Arts Council of England which enabled me to take one year off and write. I am grateful to Wolfson College, Oxford, for awarding me a Creative Arts Fellowship in Literature, which allowed me to write and research.

Contents

for Alessandro

Song of the Creatures
after St. Francis of Assisi

My good, most High, all powerful Lord,
You hold all glory, praises,
Honour, and every benediction.
Only to You these things belong,
And no man is worthy
To mention You by name.

I thank You for all of Your creation, my Lord,
Especially for brother Sun
For he is radiant, beautiful, splendid,
He gives us daylight and warmth
Bringing Your love to us.

I thank You for sister Moon and the stars,
For they are clear, precious, and beautiful
There in the sky where You placed them.

I thank You for brother Wind,
For the air and clouds, for clear weather,
For the snow and the rain
Through whom You sustain us.

I thank You for sister Water
Who is useful and humble,
Chaste and cherished.

I thank You for brother Fire
Through whom You light my road at night
For he is beautiful, playful, robust, and strong.

I thank You for mother Earth
Who governs us and nourishes us
With her fruit, herbs, flowers
And every living being.

I thank You for those who forgive
In the name of Your love,

For those who bear illnesses,
Infirmities, and suffer through hardship.
Blessed are those who endure suffering patiently
For You, my Lord, will bestow Your grace upon them.

Glory be to You, my Lord, for sister Death corporeal
From whom no living man escapes;
Forsaken are those who die in mortal sin;
Blessed are those who give themselves to You
Living by your Holy will
For them the second death will be painless.

Let us glorify, honour, and thank our Lord
Let us serve Him and His creation
With humility.

Part 1

Twenty Years

The horizon was the blue spine of a book,
its pages frozen sand, iced-over waves
and I, still unwashed of airplane fumes
day's sweat, bitterness of instant coffee,
went knee-deep in water, where I first wrote
out of my life the tangled algae of the Black Sea.

Who can see ahead on that first day when
you awake without a country, a house,
in a well-meaning stranger's bed, your
host speaking to you in an alien language?
I ate the food she served with trembling hands,
it was snowing outside, warm inside.

The following year I erased the birds: woodpecker,
sparrow, grandfather's pigeons, and the faithful stork.
In their place I wrote the hawks that scanned
the dunes of Sleeping Bear, crows, hummingbirds,
red cardinals singing
in the too-large garden of our new house.

But on this page I am leaning against lighthouses
while cherry orchards grow to the tip of Leelanau,
tree roots in water. They swish over whitened-out
cornfields of my childhood. All things I wanted to forget
crowd in-between the lines I spent years writing:
four languages, ambitions, homesickness, dispersed friends.

*

Today it is twenty years since that evening at the airport
when in blinding snow people we had not seen

were waiting for us. They said I kissed the ground.
Did I kiss the ground? Who can remember this?
We search ourselves through memories,
or autumn leaves that fall, breaking into something else.

The House of Straw

In memory of my grandparents

"In this world the house will be yours
But in the afterlife it shall be mine."
So, when they were old, they joined
In the ritual of caring for the band
Of gypsies coming through the village,
Looking after parents left by children
At empty hearths. What you give away
Stays with you in eternity,
For heaven or hell will be received
In a familiar bed, at a table you know.

Each built a separate room in the garden;
Walls and floor of new straw rugs,
A bed with a hay mattress draped in cotton,
White pillows, change of clothes,
Soft slippers to walk around the sky,
A table with chairs, a flower tapestry,
A pail filled with water from our well.
For work, each gave away bags of rice
Which needed separating grain by grain,
Beans, a sack of unsifted wheat,
Corn in a wicker basket, and two hens
To lay eggs around the house.
All other time in heaven is leisurely, they said.

*

And then, the afterlife meal:
Onions, rice, fresh tomatoes were sweated
In sunflower oil, then added to minced meat,

Flavoured with parsley and dill, some salt,
Ground pepper, an egg for binding up the mixture,
All wrapped in vine leaves stung in brine
And put to simmer all day long.
Grandmother hovered over polenta
With the wooden spoon, while buttermilk,
Aged in earthen jugs, was ready to be poured.

*

When the poor in this life were called
To receive the roofless houses of straw
Candles were lit to link living day
To other world with the cord of light;
I watched all those hands uniting
On stems of wax held at thresholds,
I saw love eternal, burning at open doors.
Then in his room, my grandfather brought
A flask of wine, set it on the table, and cried.

A Dream

You were waiting for me
To play with you as when I was a child,
Your hair, the colour of rook feathers,
Silky, almost glittery, was braided
Into two thick tails I used to envy.

I came, took off your headscarf,
And at the nape of your neck saw
Two thinning white braids
Coiled like snake-flaked skin.

I almost said "best not to return"
But did not speak a word, for you were
Studying the signs around my eyes,
That etched the sixteen years.

You remained young in my mind,
I thought the only flesh counting time
Was mine, until this dream, where
You were suddenly old.

We poured water, yeast, sugar and salt
Into flour, kneaded together the dough,
Palms and fingers focused on our ritual
Of baking bread: we were again close.

Making Wine

I.

All August we washed oak barrels
Fitted them with shiny hoops
Rolled them slowly to our well,
Filled each one to the brim,
Leaving water to swell staves.

II.

When frost fell, her elbows
White with flour sank in dough,
Round loaves baked in our clay oven,
Sheep cheese was on the table
Unwrapped from its cloth.

It was always early morning.
Blind with sleep I received
The water she poured on my hands
From the tin cup; a little chill
Came through the opened door.

Now I hear grinding of hooves,
Yoking creaks, horses breathing,
Slow rolling of wheels
On the road to the vineyard, I see
The seam of trees around our field.

III.

We each took a row: grapes hung
Heavy with sweetness, weighty, strange
With cold skin, ripeness, fragrance:

I crushed them between my palms
To show my part in harvest.

Those were long days filled with sun
Grapes in baskets, naps under oaks,
Grandparents' musings over tannin
Coating the tongue, the taste of plum
Tomatoes, sparrows diving for crumbs.

IV.
The pressing always began
With grandmother offering food
And grandfather pouring old wine
To family and neighbours, until
Red in the cheeks, we washed our feet
And went dancing in the barrel.

She in a flowery dress and
Him wearing a black suit…
I saw her return underground,
Keened the best I knew
But last time I spoke with him
He sat waiting in the quiet yard.

V.
The priest smiles as I take a mouthful
Of wine from the bottle he brought
As a wedding gift: "From your fields"
He says. I hear the clambering noise
Of time which never seemed to end
It ended, and now begins again.

Making the Hay Mattress

The best part of all that was dancing:
In August, at the summer cleaning
She threw away mattress and pillows

Stripping our bed to an idea on the empty floor,
Where, with hammer and nails she reinforced
Wobbly corners of the wooden frame.

Then in a new white case we stuffed fresh hay;
After she sealed it, she summoned us to dance
The *hora* on top to even out the surface

Soften flowers, herbs and grass.
Barefoot, we took lessons on the mattress
Stomped our feet, clapped our hands, laughed.

So it was, that till the day she died,
We danced in August and slept on flowers at night.

Summer

Once, hundreds of wild white horses galloped
On the red-painted tin-roofed house

Making me press my ears against her
Soft belly wrapped in a flower-printed dress.

Thus hail welcomed August, when she said
"Ilie, the saint, rides his chariot in the sky".

I loved being young, sitting in the shed
Next to her, waiting for the storm to pass,

Believing her stories in which she peopled
The heavens with a life just like ours.

*

This morning, far from then, there
The sky opens pages and pages of blue,

I notice that my palms are wrinkled, fine lines
Lead to the life-line: tributaries, past rains.

The willow, now almost yellow, looks
Like a middle-aged woman who has coloured

Her hair and searches for traces of beauty
In her changing face. Frost-hinting air.

Soon it will be my turn to wrap in a shawl
And think of stories to wait out thunderstorms.

Childhood Mirror

On the wall of our living room
facing the verandah
was my childhood mirror.

Twenty years ago this summer
it was a clouded retina
with milky spots, foggy patches.

If I stood in front of it now
would I see where these wrinkles
and this dusting of gray fit

on the face of that girl,
guess the absent reflections into
its foggy spots, milky patches?

Perhaps I would bow to stroke
re-imagined cheeks, hearing
a voice speaking through glass,

"You will live far from here,
I, the mirror, turn into myth
like the old well, the grape-vines

outside the window
which once I also reflected;
you too will become a story."

Harvesting Beans

The garden strewn with dry bean-
Pods rattling on their stems
As we shook them out of sacks
Onto sheets spread on the grass.

Holding thick oak sticks we sat
In a circle and beat the stalks:
Sending the freckled beans up
Free as heavy raindrops.

Grandfather waited for the wind
With instruments for sifting:
A clean straw rug, a tub-sized
Wooden bowl and a tin bucket.

That's how he remained
Pictured in my child-mind:
A shadow in the summer breeze
Standing behind the orange sun,

Hat pushed to his brow,
Hands lifting a bucket of beans,
Sounding like a downpour
As they fell, cleared of husks.

Harvesting Walnuts

Early in October, when our walnut tree
Began to drop a nut or two, here, there,
First letting go of the green husks,
With a *pluck* and a *plump* then a *thump*,

Grandfather carved sticks, thick as our arms;
We climbed the tree to knock down the walnuts:
From between leaves a bitter smell of iodine
Fell. Back on the ground we sat in a circle.

Holding round stones in yellow-stained hands
We cracked walnuts, built leaf castles
Guarded by turtle armies made of husks
And shells, and we learned the colour bitter-green.

Summer Camp

A trumpet summons them from sleep
and they run to the meadow where
small feet make big prints in the dew;

running in a circle, lifting their arms
as birds before flying, air under wings
they are doves, hummingbirds, sparrows,

chaffinches hopping
knee-deep in soft mountain fog,
in their nightgowns, summer mornings.

The Wheat Path — a Letter

red poppies
under gusts of wind
untangled from trees:

a path
in the wheat field,
the month of June up close,

flowers at my waist,
stalks against my arms
whooshing, hushing.

In that sloping land
I went back
through countries and time

to you and me, Aurora,
swearing lifelong friendship,
confiding hopes,

barefoot, outside the village.
Look here now at the two fields
juxtaposed like photograph negatives:

in one there are two girls
among stalks and flowers
dirt under our toe-nails,

our earth a gift from God.
In the other, a woman touches
the silk of a poppy to replay a memory.

Far Away

From the edge of her cornfield you could
Take the path of the weeds to the house.

Some said she was deaf, so I waited
Until I saw that she noticed my shadow.

We sat outside the whole day,
Her blue apron smelled of wild apples,

The short noon shadows around the garden
Grew tall, the gate shadow touched

Her bed of lilies, our shadows climbed
The whitewashed door, without us moving.

Once, the light of her eyes broke,
Almost tears moved across her face.

In the evening I started a fire of twigs
And she watched fireflies while I listened

To the crickets sing of summer in the grass.
There used to be days so long

I could see a thought begin on her lips
And slowly disappear into her wrinkles.

She was my silent companion,
Keeper of apples, my far away.

Piling Hay

On the field a pile, house-high, of hay,

The violinist lifted the instrument to his shoulder

Which, when we turned it in the sun to dry,

He raised the bow to the chords, drawing air in his lungs

With pitchforks and with our hands,

Summoned a song from the hollow wood,

Released a humid smell of harebells.

Gathering Wheat

Never was the end-of-summer smell
More violin-like:

From bundles of shiny, papery,
Sun-baked wheat

Piled on the straw rug in the garden,
The warm fragrance of gold seed

Tuned itself
And burned on my face.

Gypsy Woman

I

She whirled her pleated, frilled skirt
Through the wooden gates—
Red-orange-blue, dervish-woman.
She had the lips of one who lies

For happiness. A red ribbon and silver
Coins were woven in her braids.
Her beauty was her wealth,
With one gaze she charmed me.

II

After she told my fortune
She said to the wind, "Unbraid my hair,
Loosen the coins from my head, free me
From telling lies to those who need them."

So the wind wound her in his arms
As he does with the willows,
A pile of coins flickered in the sun
Then sounded on the ground like bells.

A poor prophetess without her lies,
She ran along the river.
I followed her with a good-luck
Coin pressed hard in my palm:

As we crossed the water
I forgot the fortune she told me
And, without illusions, tears
Fell to the ground like bells.

A Memory

There she is, sifting bread flour
as if enacting an apparition

in a white cloud,
in the small clay kitchen:

I take a handful of flour,
blow its dust on the floor

then make barefoot prints: from
the table towards the opened door.

Our House

When we bought the house from the village priest
Old women wrung their hands "The land is cursed":

"Stories!" my mother said, "We'll stay here.
In this place we'll build a house of dreams."

*

Two summers on my sister and I skipped on a drawing
On the ground, helped pour the foundation, ran

Alongside rising walls, making footprints and handprints,
Naming rooms and things we'd put in them.

The priest's house was a holding place, coming down
While our house grew. No one remembered the curse.

With grandparents and friends we planted
Trees, peonies, dahlias, lilies, morning glories,

A rose trellis, and one of vine bushes;
We touched every inch of land, each plant. Seasons

Yielded flowers, flowers turned to fruit, rooms were blessed
With basil, holy water, an oil candle burned facing east.

*

But it's true what they say: you can't undo the curse
On the land or the man, a cursed thing is a cursed thing.

Ten years on the house was sealed, our suitcases made
And we stood outside our own gates, agape.

Last Day in Our House

For my mother

Each, alone, walked through every room touching the walls
Sleepwalking. I shuffled along the empty hall

And pressed my lips over the fissure
Between the rocket and the star my mother painted gold,

Whispered there, "Remember me the whole of your life."
I rubbed the sweaty prints of my hands on the drawing

To leave a bit of skin on the blue whitewash,
Visible as the empty spaces where our pictures used to hang.

The Fourth Spring

From Polton to Roslin along the river
Each footstep thumps on the ceilings

Of caves, hollow but for water-sound
Blowing with the wind sweeping through trees.

And the floor of the Roslin chapel is hollow,
For I hear the shuffle of my feet in the earth.

Something pushes me on from place to place,
As if I am to check the foundations of the earth

To report on holes, gaps, emptiness, grottoes.
Like the rooms, the stone-pores, the caves

I remain half-hollow: an ear, a stethoscope
Listening for beats, pulses, skips in the land.

Cotswolds, November

When I arrived the wind
Was flattening the grass
Uprooting too the dying poplar;
Yellow lilies crowded
At the edges of the pond.

All day I stood at the window
While branches of the chestnut
Leaned and scraped the wall;
The bird's nest fell down,
Spilling little broken eggs.

In the afternoon, rain-light billowed
Over the fields. A bit of sky
Smiled in the minuscule pond
Of rainwater in the windowsill.
I liked that, and stayed a few years there.

This Moldavian Pastoral

Below the elbow of the mountain
The earth is known to hesitate, sending shivers
In the pines down the spine of the Carpathians,
Slight tremors through dreams of wolf and deer.

When they were not bee-keeping my ancestors
Bore a branch of the lime tree, or hollowed out the ash,
Glued together the opened halves into the mournful
Bucium from Vrancea women sounded over valleys.

Some days I imagine going there to rest at the pass
Across the mountain, at the seismic bend in the road
Where a gypsy band with flutes and violins will play
What they know best, until I remember my homeland.

I will say, as they say in my parts, "Tonight, *lautare*
You will be my friend and my destroyer, for I want
To drown in the music, drink the wine."
No one will know how long I have been away.

I inherited the earth's hesitation. On a monastery wall
The angel blows into the *bucium* the awakening to afterlife—
With his stork-wings, blue robes, and golden halo he
Summons the souls from earth as we did across valleys.

In this re-calling of my birth time and place
I remember the *bucium* as if it were a dream,
The angel is a projection on a school wall:
I will not return to the fault-line in the plates of the earth.

God created the heart of the earth, heal-all blue flower,
Asking it to grow as a weed on each and every road,

So if you forget to take it from Nanesti where the land
Breaks itself with sorrow, you can find it everywhere,

Even here on the banks of Cherwell, past the College gates
Where songs break out over water as you bring small
Petals, one by one, to your tongue, forgetting what it was
You wanted to say about the *bucium* from the foggy valleys.

Acciecati dalla meraviglia
(Blinded by Wonder)

Unchanged, the white curtain in the marble hall
Still half-hanging from the fallen rail

A stack of maps the child couldn't reach that first night,
Still on the gray counter-top, at the head of stairs,

The same noise from cheap shops, where they sold
Skirts and trinkets to us refugees emerging, wide-eyed

From the end of all trail-tracks at Roma Termini, and first
Memory of self with one suitcase, making a right turn

Out of the station. Then finding, as the blind does,
Whispers counting time in the ventricles

Of Santa Maria Maggiore, on each side of the nave,
From confession box to confession box.

To honour the year when we were blinded by wonder here
I walk through the same streets, revisit ancient ruins,

In a story beginning the year one hundred and six with Trajan,
I, blood of Dacian beekeeper or weapon-clad conqueror,

Shiver in the sun, not knowing what I am, as voices
From across two thousand years collect in my flesh.

After a long time

For my cousin Titi

In winter chill at the station
We pass by each other twice,
His blue eyes flicker with pain

In the stranger's face, and I look
Again beneath the layer of wrinkles,
White hair, until I find him.

Shoulder to shoulder under frescoes
For the first time in twenty years:
Each reading our lives in the paintings

For they seem to us just as invented—
I see Giotto blue with golden stars.
The Padua sky opens.

Venice

Winter tide
has drowned
marble steps.

Suddenly
off their feet,
chain-tied chairs

click-tap
in St. Mark's square
to piano and wind.

Under porticoes,
wet lovers
in rubber boots

slush-waltz;
saints in paintings
glimpse heaven

in the flooded
marbled floor
of the Basilica.

A Birthday Poem for My Father

Once upon the time he drove movie reels
Up empty roads to peasants' hamlets
Where women still wove their shirts,
Embroidered, and talked of angels.

He listened to sound of prayer bells
Starting in the hearts of wooden churches
Then rolling past haystacks in valleys,
To knock on doors nestled among trees.

Leaving a harsh father in his carpenter shop,
He talked with the wind, wandered
Alone to the other end of the country, where
He began a life of politics and prison.

He whistled through the visor in the door
In the bowels of the stone, held his vision
Above blows dealt him in torture rooms.
He owned nothing but scars when he married.

*

I see us fifteen years ago:
Helen Street, Grand Rapids, Michigan
Nights we all danced and wept with freedom,
The five of us like fingers to a hand.

He is milder with old age, smiles more,
Same stories return like old reels;
One about crossing the Iron Curtain on foot,
Another about women who loved him in Sibiu.

He drinks, makes his move on the chess-board.
I make my move and drink to him.
We toast to emptiness, to disillusion and to love.
Tomorrow we will fix the flooded basement, settle here.

Imagining the Afterlife

On a bank of the river there is a hut,
one white horse turns the lass of a well

in which she chills watermelons,
while he sleeps and their child mumbles;

a wheelbarrow filled with plum tomatoes
under the linden tree. I think they've been here

forever. Inside the house life is so simple
I thought at first it was poverty:

the kitchen stove stands on the clay floor,
hand-woven rugs cover the wicker chairs

a washing bowl is set on the table
near two plates, one glass and two spoons.

In this dream I ask both of them
if they are happy with their place in heaven:

will their house not melt if it rains?
Does God come to visit them often?

And what about me, will I have
A place at their table when the time comes.

At a Gathering of Refugees

To her it was a row of whitewashed houses
Rising from the sea; she said the whiteness
Appears and vanishes behind crests of waves.

A wooden gate with a blue rope latch
Was mine; and the path between
Pear and quince.

Neither of us named another thing
Or ate, or stayed to warm up; it was as if
Our goal was to hide our strangeness.

We both stood among
Those who owned their land, spoke
Of homelands as if they were reachable;

As if she could sail home to take her seat
At the kitchen table, begin kneading her bread.
As if I could just open the gate to my garden.

Yearning

I want to know one plot of land,
The way wrinkles begin to mould
A loved face into the scowl of its soul.

I would notice the slow knotting of trees,
How they shrivel like the skin on old hands,
Rotting of pines, the white mushroom growing

In the bruise the ivy cut in greying bark, a new
Yellow mushroom, a snail among nettles and ferns.
Climbing through the roots of fallen rhododendron

I would cling to wet earth, crawl to the place
Where rain made a face in the face of the rock,
Learn that it took years of rain and stone

Working with each other.
I would watch butterflies in the ravine
Knocked sideways by river current,

Know the times for poppies and phlox,
Wild pansies and sweet mint, the honeysuckle leaning in
From hedges, the day when the dog rose blooms.

But in the promised-land
The silver maple digs its roots under the porch,
And moles dig our crops out of the earth.

The Names of Things

Sunlight in a water bowl on the doorstep
Then on a pond far from home: *soarele.*

Fire in the terracotta hearth, then
In a pit, outside a tent, thousands of miles away: *focul.*

My Black Sea lulling the shore, then dreams
Of sea waking cheeks with stinging salt: *marea.*

Air encircling the grapes outside the window,
Then gliding with a parachute above a heron: *aerul.*

Soil exhaling after rain through gaps between cherry leaves,
Then crying dirty tears from roots of a fallen birch: *pamintul.*

Naframa

for Loredana and Dean

In our parts, one week before the wedding
The wife-to-be embroiders a white cloth

With flowers which gather in the shape
Of cross when the cloth is folded.

The newlyweds place it above the icon of the house
Where it slowly yellows with time.

Half is torn upon the death of the first spouse
The other half stays with the one left behind

So in the afterlife lovers will find one
Another by the flowers on their *naframa*.

Sister, anchored to its half-remembered origins,
The heart of marriage sways around the myth again,
Today for you and your crowned heads.

On a Ten-Year Wedding Anniversary

For Jessica and Jeff

Here, half-gone autumn over treetops.
Up the mountain the snow has settled
already: a swan beginning to nest.

Today the seasons are mixed in my mind:
that afternoon when we planted flowers,
gathered forgotten, other years' leaves

then went to the village to be by ourselves.
How you come to me now like a pair of hands
rising from chest towards the lips!

Who can say what love is, where it comes from
or where it goes; maybe it was there
before we were born, waiting for our hands.

In our hands it took flesh, planted
peonies, gathered dead leaves left by those
from whom we bought this house. It sings in our children.

The diamond ring arrived yesterday, ten years on—
a messenger through time, light of a star
burning since long ago, reaching us.

Letter

for Catalin

Second day of frost makes dahlias around the lake look old.
The willow bows over the bank with loosened hair,
Off-course geese land on water sending spouts over cattails,
The sun rises from behind a clump of leafless birches, white:
Any other day, I would just say it feels a slightly melancholy day.

I remember being young, hearing about you lying crosswise
In our mother's womb, then horizontally, vertically, moving
Until the birth, when you came to this world with broken shoulders
And a bluish face; it took years to make you strong. You were
The light to which our faces turned morning after morning.

Ulysses had seen fantastic worlds and returned:
Now you need to go away, so you can have your journey home.
Go with masts built of our love: may your sails be strong
May the Atlantic, Euphrates and Tigris be gentle to you,
Return to us easily and surely as the light of day returns.

Any other day, I would just say it feels a slightly melancholy day
But your leaving the house, my brother, is taking the windows
With you, the walls, crossbeams, leaving the roof
Supported by the plangent, fragile, prayerful soul of hope;
Frost on the grass, water in the lake, geese in the weeds

Weep. Your return shall be happiness, walls of house,
Windows in walls, sun through windows
And my heart will brim over with words of thanksgiving.

The Heron

Wide wings
Rose from the river

Leaves
  quivered,
White
blooms
  fell

A gap of air
Went up with her

Leaving me

A channel from
Dreaming to waking.

She flew so closely above,
I shivered.

The Rook

The whole month of June I saw
How with broken claw and wings,
It called to the forest, refused strawberries,
Kept towards the canopy of trees.

Then the fifth Sunday came,
We lifted the cage, bidding it farewell.
Tar-black, it flapped quickly, flew
In a circle as if to take off, then fell.

*

He said he stood outside the gates
Until they sent him with the first train.
There, in that station where convicts
Come and go, he cried, a free man.

Part 2

A Sort of Question

for Alessandro

The wind has swept all day through the garden;
Pelted the statues by the well with blown petals
Until their seclusion in the wall was colored in,
Their embracing gaze revealed.

The gardener took off his shirt and waded
Into the stream of hay beyond the cave wall.
A bee came through my window like a missile,
Then buzzed, confused, on the vase of foxgloves.
So much sun there was it held me still.

I watched for signs and portents all day long:
A blown branch could be a broken promise,
A sudden change of weather, a change of heart,
But there was nothing, only summer, wildly
Working inside trees, wind pouncing on glass.

Mating Swans

She stood still in the centre of the lake,
Head high, raised tail, white calligraphy.

He made a clock on the face of water
Arresting the sun, her gaze and the reeds.

From the tongue of twelve o'clock he
Bowed before her, a question mark

And she answered with her own bow,
A question, before him: turn following

Turn. When he mounted her
I called you and we blushed together

Through their dance of coiling necks,
Kissing beaks, beating wings.

At the end two questions faced each other
Raising a heart on their bed of water.

We too, that morning, bowed
And drew on our blue cotton sheets.

Fishing in the North Esk

for Roland

It wasn't trout fighting in the mouth
Of the bear, camera batteries
Jumping from their holster,

Scrambling up bank through flinty
Rocks hidden in the cover of moss
Running for our lives from the hungry beast,

Not even the scientifically-engineered sheep
From the next field making an appearance
With tails in their heads or stuff like that.

No: it was the sky at six in the morning
A little net we did not know how to use
And the casting of fly in tree branches;

As we stumbled over pebbles laughing,
Posed for camera with practiced expressions,
The trout slept peacefully in North Esk.

We returned home carrying in our minds
One view of the river widening
Into the valley, singing where we stood,

A memory of a golden ladder, lodged among
Red rocks underwater, and a foxglove growing
On the bank like a vine filled with red bells.

Loss

When the winter moon made a half turn
You struck your first notes in my womb.

I carried home an armful of tulips.
In their softness I imagined you.

How you brought all the words back to me
Cantarea, iubirea, familia, nasterea!

*

Above the mud-colored pond, the sun
Spits bits of gold through ruptured clouds

Last night you uprooted yourself from me;
A song struggling inside an instrument.

How everything is gone with you
As in a dream I am no longer sure I had.

Versailles, the Hall of Mirrors

What wasn't draped for restoration,
Flickered with the two of them,
The way eyes sparkle back at things:
Two hands playing in the image of the fountain
Reflected in one mirror, a quick kiss
On one corner of his lips,
The slow caress his fingers
Traced on her left wrist,

Spied and caught in the permanence of marble.

Sure there is more to the Hall of Mirrors
Than married flirtation on a workday,
But that's how life burst in a neglected room:
Right there, with the old sun skidding
From one mirror to the next, his chest
Multiplied into a thousand and one
Chests for her to lay her head on.

Morning at Esthwaite Lake

Her child turns inside the womb
Quickening her heart; it is
A half-heard song reaching across
Water through noise of waves.

These are still the small hours.
There is only a hint of sky now.
Esthwaite lies covered in fog.
She thinks of fish turning under.

Flowers on the table wait
Their color from daylight.
Half-clothed in clouds distant hills
Appear; husband's bare shoulders,

Resting over sheets. The child kicks
She settles at the window and waits.
Soon there will be a rainbow
With one foot in the water.

From the Beginning

The river shimmers under the bridge;
Scales on the back of fish.
Broken ice in the pond glitters,
Life grows inside of me, prepares.

Now that I know you are
Moving and growing,
I make one cross with holy oil
On my belly and one on my chest

So we can breathe together
And borrow dreams from each other:
Me, your unborn imaginings about
World and sun waiting for you.

You, my blood in which I send you
Fresh food and words,
So when you join us here,
By the water, we can talk.

First Born

for Stefano

You are calling of the *toaca*
And cliff-growing vineyards above the sea.
I whirl and cradle you among the stars.

Outside the walls of my skin Segovia plays his guitar
To winter wind in a country which is not his nor ours.
You quicken to the wind-knock on the window, I answer.

I talk with hares and crows night after night
Worrying they have come to take you from me,
Now I know all languages, I fight with spirits about the yard.

You love the sound of this world, the light of sun
The strings of guitar, the way voices of people
Sound warm, welcoming you, so you come

Blood-bathed. A warrior. I lie: Milky Way
On a clear night. You are no longer a secret.
Now take me inside your smile, child, sing me to sleep.

The Two of Us

for Stefano

Here we are, face to face
Trying out your first words:

You point, exclaim,
And I look again,

To see how things
Hold their new names.

My little brown-eyed
Golden hair, dimples

In the cheeks angel:
How shall I describe you?

Abundance

for Lucy

That summer pears were
bruised from plumpness,
ripeness, on thick cool grass
under the tree.

The whole time over our tea
above rooftops,
in the study with sky windows,
I kept thinking "Ask for a pear,

maybe that blushed one, big as two
cupped hands, by the wooden gate".
I asked and you set it on the table
where it glowed in its own image.

We talked and talked.
Forgot the pear there
the way one forgets to open
a letter long waited for.

While Chasing Rainbows

for Alisa

Thirteen months I waited for the right sky
To describe how I felt when you were born,

And here it is, this morning, out of the blue:
White, gray, and deep blue clouds, hang low,

A row of pearls on the soft Jura, so low
You can see the gentle mountain top in clear sunshine

And worry that somehow the sky is going to fall
On earth, leaving Mt. Blanc in opposite direction

Suspended in the air, spoon-like and white,
Like some kind of fault in vision.

And then, a dust of first snow, an apparition,
Suddenly illuminated by a rainbow

So clear—from St. Jean de Gonville
To Col de la Faucille—I change direction

And we drive straight into it, as if we're
Going through Heaven's Arch. But it's more:

Another rainbow and another, and another yet,
All day rise and paint the mountain air

With the kind of joy that makes me forget where I am
Going and why. And you are crying in the backseat

As babies do, hungry for breast, comfort, and love.
The day when you arrived it was just like that,

One burst of nature happening after another, mid morning,
Turning the whole morning right around, feet tiptoeing the
        birthing sky

And at eleven and one minute you were landed
On my startled chest. I was still waiting to give birth to you.

The Coming of Winter

Suddenly trees struggle
with weight of fruit; under branches
the earth is red with apples.

Pears reach our shoulders. It is all
but September, I grip the last hours
of summer; roses are still opening.

Silver maple leaves; gray in my hair.

There

A drop of water on water:
        there
a circle opens slowly
this is your life.

Part 3

Night Tempest

The wind *rasps* at shutters,
Clears trees out of its throat, coughs leaves
Rattles stones in its lungs, spitting small whistles
That skid on the windowsill, wheezes twigs
On the driveway, blows the willow sideways.

The house that I built with my child hands
Crumbles again in my dreams and as always
I hang on to the roof that faces the side of the church
That shows Mary and Joseph sharing the burden of Jesus
With their donkey and walking stick.

Lac Léman, startled from its night-blue rest,
Throws boats on the shore, masts break on sidewalks—
Giant pencils—in the morning we'll find them frozen
On the grass, over chestnut branches and benches,
Like evidence of recurring dreams in the tired light of eyes.

Visiting the Country of My Birth

The tyrant and his wife were exhumed
For proper burial; it is twenty years since
They were shot against a wall in Christmas snow.

*

The fish in the Black Sea are dead. Waves roll them
To the beach. Tractors comb the sand. We stand at water's edge
Whispering, glassy-eyed, throats parched from heat.

Stray dogs howl through nights like choirs
Of mutilated angels, circle around us on hill paths,
Outside gas stations, shops, streets, in parking lots.

Farther, into wilderness, we slow down where horse
And foal walk home to the clay hut by themselves,
Cows cross roads in evenings alone, bells clinking.

People sit on wooden benches in front of their houses,
Counting hours until darkness, while
Shadows of mountains caress their heads.

On through hot dust of open plane, to my village:
A toothless man from twenty years ago
Asks for money, says he used to work for us.

*

I am searching for prints of mare's hooves in our yard
Between stable and kitchen window, now gone
With the time my two feet used to fit inside one hoof.

We sit down to eat on the porch when two sparrows
Come flying in circles over the table, low and fast, happily!
"My grandparents' souls" I think aloud, but my cousin says:

"No, the sparrows have nested under eaves, look
Past the grapevine." Nests big as cupped hands, twigs
And straw. Bird song skids in the air above us.

Into still-remaining rooms no sewing machine,
Or old furniture with sculpted flowers on walnut wood.
No rose bushes climbing window sills, outside.

And here, our water well, a vase of cracked cement. Past
Ghosts of lilac, pear, and quince in the sun-bitten yard I step
On re-imagined hooves, pull the chain, smell wet rust.

Unblemished sky ripples inside the tin bucket,
Cradled in my arms the way I used to hold
Warm goose eggs close to skin so not to break them:

"The earth will remember you" my grandparents once said.
 Here, where such dreams do not come true, I have come
To find hoof-prints as well as signs from sparrows.

The Latch

Glimmers in their worn-out eyes
Suddenly alive! Old neighbours
Straighten up, stand in plastic sandals.

Once, their taut skin
On hay-lifting arms, faces shining
The way wealth does, fetchingly.

They look unbelievingly, for
The girl with readable eyes has returned
Inside someone they cannot touch.

*

Outside the gates of the house I built as a child
(that summer coming back now...
game of making a pretend-life out of clay),

I do not lift the latch, sensing the scarred earth
From which the apple tree was torn,
Wounds in soil from where the grape vine

Trellis was uprooted. Startled black loam.
Sacred dust sticks to our feet, white sandals,
The boy—just taller than his tin bucket—stoops

Under weight of water by the well,
Then walks, leaving a trail on the dirt road
Like me once, glad, and sad, for water-spill.

Here, inside their eyes, wide as
Garden plots where you can grow enough.
So this shall be my salvation.

Notes

P.9   SONG OF THE CREATURES
'*Cantico Delle Creature*' by San Francesco di Assisi, *1226 AD*

P.15   THE HOUSE OF STRAW
This poem describes *grijirea*, a ritual practised around the villages in the Moldavian region of Romania to prepare people for the afterlife.

p.20   MAKING THE HAY MATTRESS
The *hora* is a Moldavian dance.

P.36   THIS MOLDAVIAN PASTORAL
The *bucium* is a wind instrument of about 1.5–3 meters in length; it is made of ash, maple, lime or hazel wood which is bored, slit lengthways, hollowed out and then glued together.

A *lautare* is a village musician, usually playing the fiddle.

p.46   THE NAMES OF THINGS
Soarele, focul, marea, aerul, pamintul are: sun, fire, sea, air, earth.

p.48   ON A TEN-YEAR WEDDING ANIVERSARY
Naframa is a traditional Romanian wedding gift.

p.58   LOSS
Cantarea, iubirea, familia, nasterea are: song, love, family, birth.

P.62   FIRST BORN
Toaca is a Romanian Orthodox prayer bell made of wood.

Lightning Source UK Ltd.
Milton Keynes UK
UKOW03f0004120214

226312UK00001B/210/P